American Girl®

Cooking

Photography **Nicole Hill Gerulat**

weldon**owen**

Contents

Main Dishes

Side Dishes

Cook Up Some Fun!

Being able to cook the food you love to eat is a skill you can have fun with your entire life. You'll be able to make what you want when you want to eat it, and the results will be better for you than food you buy already prepared. With this book as your very own cooking coach, you'll learn how to make delicious snacks, soups, salads, main dishes, and sides not only for yourself but for your friends and family, too!

Any time you work in the kitchen, a parent or other adult should be around to help. But even so, you'll feel a great sense of independence and accomplishment knowing you can create an amazing meal from scratch. You'll also discover that cooking is an activity where you can let your creativity flow. And it's an excellent way to spend time with friends and family.

Whether you want to make yummy treats for a sleepover, cook a special meal for your family, or just have fun and learn some new skills in the kitchen, this book has you covered. Maybe you like to follow a recipe step-by-step so the results are always familiar, or maybe you're the kind of cook who likes to add your own pizzazz to a dish to make it uniquely yours. With these recipes, you can create your own style of cooking and let your personality shine. So go ahead—flip through the pages, bookmark some delish dishes, and get ready to make food that'll have your pals saying "OMG, yum!"

Feast like you mean it!

In these pages, you'll find recipes for irresistible snacks like Sweet-n-Salty Popcorn (page 19), which is perfect for movie night, and Fruit & Granola Bars (page 34), for eating on the go. Lunch gets a fab upgrade with dishes like BLT Salad with Avocado (page 45), Greek Salad Pitas (page 40), and Creamy Tomato Soup with Cheese Toasts (page 54). And for dinner, there's even more yumminess to come! Impress your family and friends with Rosemary Roast Chicken (page 75) or Baked Penne with Spinach & Cheese (page 96). And don't forget the side dishes! Bet you can't eat just one of the Sweet Potato Chips (page 101), and everyone will be saying "Mmmmm" when they try a slice of Cheesy Garlic Bread (page 102).

All of the recipes in this book are ideal for sharing, so host a special dinner, a pizza party, a potluck, a birthday bash, or any kind of get-together that reflects your own style and serve up some of your new favorite dishes.

Cooking with care

When you see this symbol in the book, it means that you need an adult to help you with all or part of the recipe. Ask for help before continuing.

Adults have lots of culinary wisdom, and they can help keep you safe in the kitchen. Always have an adult assist you, especially if your recipe involves high heat, sharp objects, and electric appliances. Be sure to wash your hands before you begin cooking and after touching raw meat, poultry, eggs, or seafood.

Tip-top cooking tips

WATCH THE HEAT

Stovetop burners, hot ovens, boiling water—there's a lot of heat involved in cooking, so it's important to be careful when working in the kitchen. Always use oven mitts when handling hot equipment, and have an adult help you when you're cooking at the stovetop, moving things in and out of the oven, and working with hot liquids or foods.

GET HELP WITH SHARP TOOLS

Soon you'll be chopping, slicing, and mincing, but before you start, make sure an adult is there to help you choose the correct knife (not too big, but not too small either), and be sure to hold the knife firmly at the base. When you're not using the knife, place it somewhere safe so it can't fall on the floor or be reached by younger siblings.

STAY ORGANIZED

Staying organized and paying attention are important cooking skills. Before you fire up the stovetop or oven, read the recipe, including the ingredient list, from start to finish. Then it's time to clear a clean surface and lay out all your cooking tools and ingredients. Once the food starts cooking, be sure to set a timer!

The tools you'll need

The recipes in this book use a few basic cooking tools. There's no need to go out and buy everything all at once—you can collect tools slowly over time, as you try your hand at different recipes and styles of cooking.

★ **An apron** is handy to help keep your clothes tidy when you are cooking.

★ **A baking sheet** is great for cooking food in the oven. The big, flat surface of a baking sheet lets you spread out ingredients like cauliflower or potatoes into a single layer so they cook quickly and evenly. You can line the baking sheet with aluminum foil or parchment paper to prevent food from sticking and to make cleanup a snap.

★ **A food processor** is a small electric appliance that comes with different blades and disks that can slice, chop, purée, and shred ingredients. It can also knead dough. Ask an adult for help when using a food processor and be careful of the sharp blades.

★ **Frying pans and sauté pans** are shallow pans with sloped or straight sides. They can be used for sautéing, stir-frying, and pan-frying. A nonstick pan helps prevent food from sticking and makes cleanup easier.

★ **A ladle** is a long-handled spoon with a cup-like bowl. It's used for serving sauces and soups from deep pots.

★ **Measuring cups and spoons** help you measure your ingredients accurately and easily. Choose graduated sets for dry ingredients and a liquid pitcher for wet ingredients.

★ **Oven mitts or pads** protect your hands from hot pans, oven racks, baking sheets, and baking dishes.

★ **A rubber spatula** is helpful for mixing and for scraping foods out of bowls or pans, like when you transfer hummus from the food processor to a serving bowl. Wide, flat metal spatulas are used to flip food over during cooking.

★ **Saucepans** are deep pots with long handles and lids used for stovetop cooking, such as boiling and simmering. They come in different sizes—small ones hold 1 to 2 quarts, medium ones hold 2 to 3 quarts, and large ones hold about 4 quarts.

Many of the recipes in this book can be customized to include your favorite flavors. Add some personal flair to every dish!

Snacks

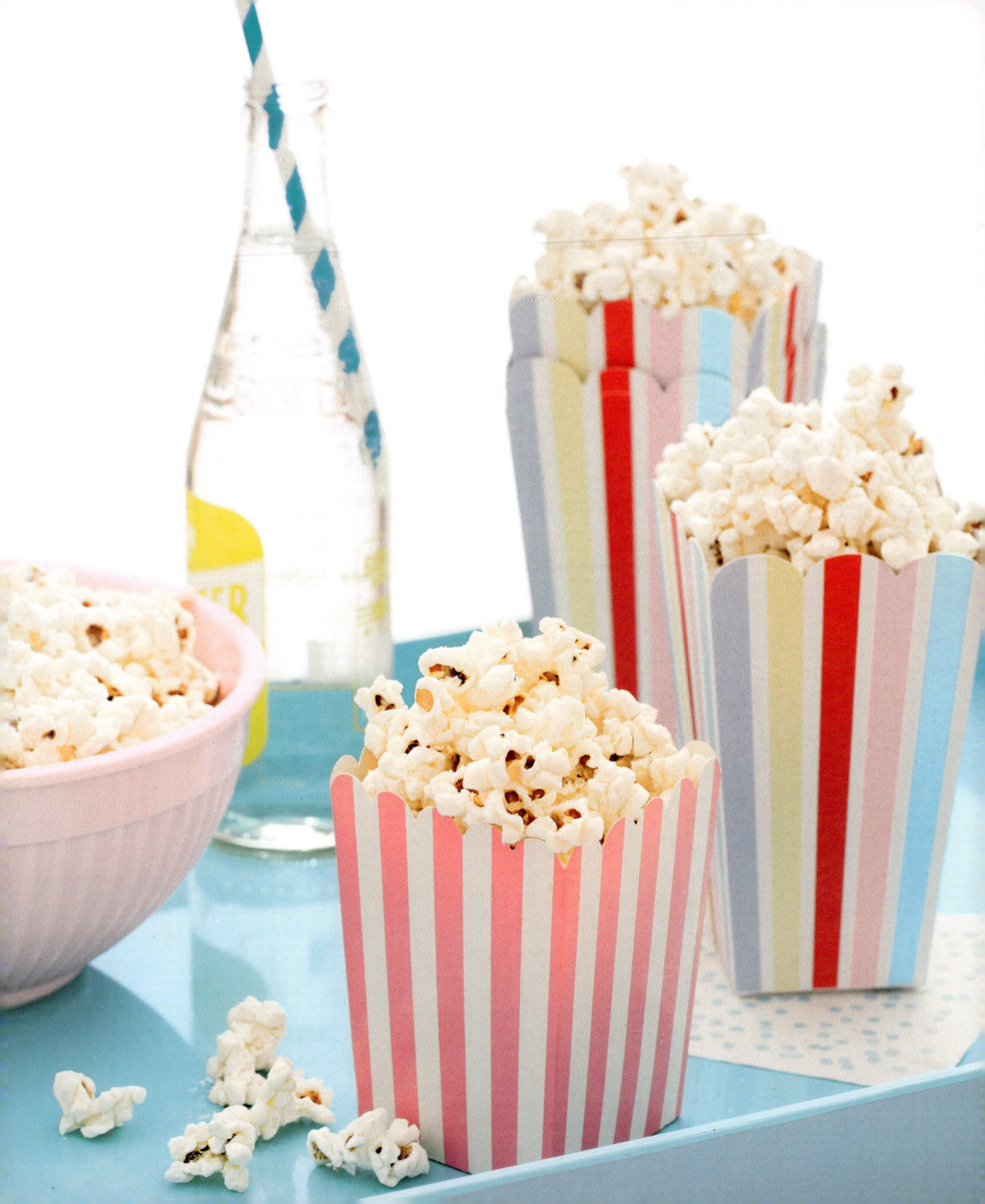

Sweet-n-Salty Popcorn

Two kinds of popcorn—one a little sweet, one a little savory—ensures that everyone gets their favorite snack for your next movie night. Put the popcorn in cute bags or boxes and give each person their own, or just serve it in two bowls and let everyone share!

MAKES 4 SERVINGS

¼ cup canola oil

½ cup popcorn kernels

3 teaspoons salt

¼ cup powdered sugar

1 cup grated Parmesan cheese

3 tablespoons unsalted butter, melted

Pour the canola oil into a large, heavy saucepan. Set the pan over medium heat, add the popcorn, and cover. Cook, shaking the pan often, until you hear kernels popping. Continue to cook, shaking the pan continuously, until the popping slows to 3 to 5 seconds between pops. Remove the pan from the heat, carefully lift off the lid, and divide the popcorn evenly between 2 bowls.

Sprinkle 2 teaspoons of the salt and the powdered sugar over 1 bowl of popcorn. Sprinkle the cheese, butter, and remaining 1 teaspoon salt over the second bowl.

Using clean hands or a large spoon, toss the popcorn in each bowl until well combined. Scoop the popcorn into individual bags or boxes—sweet in one and cheesy in another—and serve right away.

BOYLAN

Caprese Kebabs

These cute skewers put all the flavors of caprese salad on a stick! Use multicolored cherry tomatoes for extra fun, and omit the basil if you don't like it. Make sure you toast your bread until it's golden, but not too crisp or the cubes will be hard to skewer.

MAKES 12 KEBABS

12 wooden skewers

Three or four 1-inch-thick slices crusty country-style bread, such as Italian or sourdough

2 tablespoons olive oil

Salt

24 cherry tomatoes

24 small fresh basil leaves

24 small fresh mozzarella balls

Preheat the oven to 400°F.

Trim the crusts off of the bread and cut the slices into twenty-four 1-inch cubes. Transfer the cubes to a rimmed baking sheet and drizzle with 1 tablespoon of the olive oil. Sprinkle with a little salt, toss to combine, and spread the cubes into an even layer. Bake, stirring once halfway through, until the bread is golden, about 10 minutes. Remove the baking sheet from the oven and let the bread cool completely.

Onto each wooden skewer, thread 2 bread cubes, 2 tomatoes, 2 basil leaves, and 2 mozzarella balls in any order that you like. Place the skewers on a serving dish and drizzle with the remaining 1 tablespoon olive oil. Sprinkle with a little salt and serve right away.

Deviled Eggs

Creamy, tangy deviled eggs are a party favorite. You can personalize them by adding 1 teaspoon pickle relish or grated lemon zest and chopped fresh parsley to the yolk mixture. If you want to get fancy, use a piping bag with a star tip to pipe the yolk mixture.

MAKES 4 SERVINGS

4 large eggs

2 tablespoons mayonnaise

½ teaspoon Dijon mustard

Salt and ground black pepper

Sweet paprika

Gently place the eggs in a medium saucepan and fill the pan with enough cold water to cover the eggs. Set the pan over medium heat. When the water bubbles gently, reduce the heat to low and cook for 15 minutes.

Fill a medium bowl with cold water. Using a slotted spoon, carefully remove the eggs from the pan and place them in the bowl. Let the eggs sit in the water for 10 minutes. Replace with new cold water, if necessary, until the eggs are cool to the touch.

Remove the eggs from the water. Gently tap each one against the work surface and roll it back and forth under your hand, applying light pressure, to crack the shell all over. Carefully peel off the shell.

Cut each egg in half lengthwise. Use a spoon to scoop the yolks out of the egg whites and put them in a small bowl. Place the egg-white halves on a serving platter.

Add the mayonnaise and mustard to the yolks. Use the spoon to mash them to a paste. Season to taste with salt and pepper.

Spoon the yolk mixture into the egg-white halves, dividing it evenly and forming it into a mound. Sprinkle each mound with a pinch of paprika. Serve right away.

Guacamole & Star Chips

Avocados, the main ingredient in guacamole, are not only good for you, they're creamy and scrumptious! This much-loved dip is perfect for a party. If you make your guac in advance, squeeze a little extra lime juice over the top.

MAKES 6 SERVINGS

1 large ripe tomato

3 ripe avocados

Juice of 2 limes

Salt

2 green onions, finely chopped (optional)

½ teaspoon ground cumin (optional)

2 tablespoons chopped fresh cilantro

Tortilla chips for serving (for Star Chips, see Note at right)

Insert the tip of a paring knife into the top of the tomato, just outside of the spot where the stem was attached, and cut around that spot, removing the tough core. Put the tomato on its side and cut it in half crosswise. Use a small spoon to scoop out the seeds from each half. Discard the seeds. Cut each tomato half lengthwise into thin slices. A few at a time, gather the slices into a bundle and cut them crosswise to form small, even cubes. Put the tomatoes in a medium bowl.

Cut the avocados in half lengthwise around the large pits in the centers. Twist the halves in opposite directions to separate them. Using a spoon, scoop out the pits and discard them, and then scoop the avocado flesh out of each half into the bowl with the tomatoes. Add the juice of 1½ limes, ½ teaspoon salt, the green onions (if using), and the cumin (if using) to the avocado mixture. Use a potato masher or fork to mash everything to a chunky paste. Stir in the cilantro. Taste the guacamole and, if you like, stir in more lime juice and salt. Serve with tortilla chips for dipping.

Star Chips Preheat the oven to 350°F. Using a 3-inch star-shaped cookie cutter, cut stars out of six 6-inch corn tortillas (you should get 3 from each tortilla). Lightly grease 2 baking sheets with canola oil, then place the stars on the baking sheets so that they are not overlapping. Bake until brown around the edges, 8 to 10 minutes. Let the chips cool slightly, then transfer to a platter and serve.

Griddled Corn Fritters with Lime

These are made best with fresh corn in the summer, but thawed frozen corn kernels will work, too. For a twist, mix in 1 teaspoon each finely chopped green onion and chopped fresh cilantro and ¼ cup shredded Cheddar cheese with the corn.

MAKES 24 FRITTERS

1½ cups fresh corn kernels (from about 3 ears) or thawed frozen corn kernels, chopped

2 teaspoons fresh lime juice

1 large egg

½ cup whole milk

2 tablespoons unsalted butter, melted and cooled

¾ cup all-purpose flour

¼ cup fine-grind cornmeal

1 teaspoon baking powder

½ teaspoon salt

Canola oil for deep-frying

Lime wedges for serving

In a small bowl, stir together the corn kernels and lime juice (the lime juice actually makes the corn taste sweeter). In a medium bowl, whisk together the egg, milk, and butter until blended. In a large bowl, stir together the flour, cornmeal, baking powder, and salt. Pour the egg mixture into the flour mixture and mix until smooth. Stir in the corn.

Put a wire rack on a large rimmed baking sheet and place the baking sheet near the stove. Pour canola oil into a deep, heavy saucepan to a depth of 1 inch. Set the pan over medium-high heat and warm the oil until it reaches 375°F on a deep-frying thermometer.

Scoop up a heaping tablespoon of batter and very gently add the batter to the hot oil, being careful not to let it splash. Repeat to form more fritters, but don't crowd the pan. Fry the fritters until browned on the bottom, about 2 minutes. Using a slotted spoon, flip the fritters and fry until golden on both sides, puffed, and cooked through, 2 to 3 minutes longer. Using the slotted spoon, transfer them to the wire rack to drain. Fry more fritters in the same way until all of the batter is used up.

Serve right away with lime wedges for squeezing.

Lemony Hummus

Hummus is a snap to make in a food processor. Try puréeing a roasted red pepper or drained oil-packed sun-dried tomatoes with the chickpeas for a tasty twist. Serve hummus with veggie sticks, pita chips, or mini pita breads.

MAKES 6-8 SERVINGS

1 clove garlic, peeled and chopped

One 15-ounce can chickpeas, rinsed and drained

Salt

Water

⅓ cup well-stirred tahini (sesame paste)

1 tablespoon olive oil

Juice of 2 lemons

Put the garlic, chickpeas, ½ teaspoon salt, and 6 tablespoons water in a food processor and cover. Process the mixture for 1 minute. Turn off the machine and scrape down the sides with a rubber spatula. Replace the lid and purée again until the mixture is smooth, about 1 minute. Add the tahini, olive oil, and lemon juice and blend for another minute. If the mixture is very thick, add more water, 1 teaspoon at a time, and process until well combined. Taste the hummus and blend in more salt if you think it needs it.

Using the rubber spatula, scrape the hummus into a bowl. Serve right away or cover the bowl with plastic wrap and refrigerate for up to 3 days.

Hot Cheese Dip

With two kinds of cheese, this ooey-gooey dip will be the hit of your next party! Swap out crackers for the baguette, and if you like, serve up some sliced apples and steamed broccoli florets for dipping, too.

MAKES **8** SERVINGS

2 cups shredded Gruyère cheese

2 cups shredded fontina cheese or Swiss cheese

2 tablespoons cornstarch

½ cup low-sodium vegetable or chicken broth

½ cup water

2 tablespoons apple cider vinegar

1 small clove garlic, smashed

1 baguette, cut into cubes, for serving

Place the cheeses in a 1-gallon zipper-lock plastic bag. Add the cornstarch, seal the bag, and shake until well mixed.

In a medium saucepan, combine the vegetable broth, water, vinegar, and garlic. Set the pan over medium-high heat and bring the liquid to a boil. Reduce the heat to medium, add a handful of the cheese mixture to the broth mixture, and whisk until the cheese is almost fully melted. Repeat with the remaining cheese mixture, adding it handful by handful and whisking until smooth after each addition. After you've added all the cheese, keep whisking until the mixture starts to bubble, about 1 minute longer. Remove and discard the garlic clove.

Transfer the cheese dip to a warmed serving bowl or a fondue pot with a heat source underneath. Serve right away with the baguette slices and with fondue forks for spearing and dunking the bread.

Fruit & Granola Bars

These granola bars taste way better than anything you can buy at the store. Substitute your favorite nuts and dried fruits for the ones listed below, but make sure the nuts you use are raw, not roasted or toasted, since they will cook in the oven.

MAKES 16 BARS

3 tablespoons unsalted butter, plus more for greasing the baking dish

2 cups old-fashioned rolled oats

1 cup raw whole almonds

½ cup raw pumpkin seeds (pepitas)

¼ cup raw sunflower seeds

½ cup dried currants or raisins

½ cup dried cranberries

⅔ cup honey

¼ cup firmly packed light brown sugar

1 teaspoon vanilla extract

¼ teaspoon salt

Preheat the oven to 350°F. Butter a 9-by-13-inch baking dish and line it with parchment paper, extending the paper up and over the sides on two sides. Butter the paper.

On a rimmed baking sheet, combine the oats, almonds, pumpkin seeds, and sunflower seeds. Bake, stirring once or twice, just until golden, about 8 minutes. Remove the baking sheet from the oven and transfer the mixture to a large bowl. Stir in the currants and cranberries and set aside. Reduce the oven temperature to 300°F.

In a small saucepan, combine the butter, honey, sugar, vanilla, and salt. Set the pan over medium heat and bring the mixture to a boil, stirring often. Cook for about 30 seconds, or until the butter is fully melted. Pour the mixture over the oat mixture and stir gently until evenly moistened. Scoop the mixture into the prepared baking dish and let cool slightly.

Using dampened hands, press the mixture into an even layer. Bake until golden around the edges, about 20 minutes. Set the baking dish on a wire rack and let cool for 10 minutes. Using the parchment paper as handles, lift the granola out of the pan and place it directly on the rack. Let cool completely.

Transfer the granola onto a cutting board. To cut the bars, make 3 evenly spaced lengthwise cuts and 3 evenly spaced crosswise cuts across the granola. Serve the bars right away or store them in an airtight container for up to 5 days.

Soups & Salads

Add pizzazz
Make the guac with star chips (page 26) and serve with this taco-licious salad for a star-rific presentation.

Taco Salad

A towering taco salad with seasoned beef, beans, and cheese makes a hearty and super-tasty lunch. Serve each portion in a bowl-shaped fried corn tortilla for a really festive presentation.

MAKES **4** SALADS

1 pound ground beef

¼ cup taco seasoning mix

⅔ cup water

1 ripe avocado

½ head iceberg lettuce, shredded

2 plum tomatoes, chopped

1 cup canned black beans or pinto beans, rinsed and drained

1½ cups shredded Monterey jack cheese or Cheddar cheese

Your favorite salsa

1 lime cut into 4 wedges

Tortilla chips for serving

Put the ground beef in a large frying pan. Set the pan over medium heat. Cook the meat, breaking up clumps with a wooden spoon, until browned, 8 to 10 minutes. If the beef looks greasy, pour off and discard the fat in the pan. Stir in the taco seasoning and water, raise the heat to high, and bring to a boil. Reduce the heat to low and simmer, stirring often, until the liquid is gone, about 12 minutes.

While the meat is cooking, cut the avocado in half lengthwise around the large pit in the center. Twist the halves in opposite directions to separate them. Using a spoon, scoop out the pit and discard it. Carefully peel the skin off each half, and then cut the avocado into ½-inch cubes.

Divide the lettuce among 4 plates. Top each with equal amounts of the tomatoes, beans, and avocado.

When the meat is done, use a slotted spoon to divide it evenly among the salads, and then sprinkle the cheese on top. Spoon some salsa onto each salad. Serve with the lime wedges for squeezing and tortilla chips alongside.

Greek Salad Pitas

You can turn these stuffed pita sandwiches into wraps by using flour tortillas, Indian naan, or even lavash. Just roll up the filling and take it to go! Try adding some thinly sliced red onion or slivers of red bell pepper.

MAKES 4 SERVINGS

2 regular or whole-wheat pita breads

1 cup chopped romaine lettuce

¼ English cucumber, peeled and chopped

1 large plum tomato, chopped

2 tablespoons chopped pitted black olives (optional)

2 tablespoons crumbled feta cheese or goat cheese

1 tablespoon olive oil

2 teaspoons balsamic or red wine vinegar

Salt

¼ cup Lemony Hummus (page 32) or store-bought hummus

1 cup chopped or shredded cooked chicken

Preheat the oven to 400°F.

Stack the pita breads and cut them in half. Wrap the halves in aluminum foil. Place in the oven to warm for 5 minutes.

Meanwhile, in a medium bowl, combine the lettuce, cucumber, tomato, olives (if using), and cheese. In a small bowl, whisk together the olive oil and vinegar, season with salt, and then drizzle the mixture over the salad. Using tongs, toss to combine.

Remove the pita breads from the oven and unwrap them. Spread the inside of each pita with 1 tablespoon hummus. Add the chicken, dividing evenly. Spoon the salad inside, dividing it evenly. Serve right away.

BLT Salad with Avocado

This recipe turns a classic sandwich into a chunky, colorful salad. Bacon, lettuce, red and yellow tomatoes, crunchy bread, and avocado are topped off with a creamy, lemony dressing. Yum!

MAKES 4 SERVINGS

DRESSING

½ cup sour cream

2 tablespoons fresh lemon juice

2 tablespoons grated Parmesan cheese

1 clove garlic, chopped

¼ teaspoon salt

SALAD

8 slices thick-cut bacon

4 thick slices crusty country-style bread, such as Italian or sourdough, cut into cubes

2 tablespoons olive oil

Salt

1 ripe avocado

1 large or 2 medium hearts of romaine lettuce, chopped

1 cup red cherry tomatoes, halved

1 cup yellow cherry tomatoes, halved

Preheat the oven to 400°F.

To make the dressing, combine the sour cream, lemon juice, Parmesan, garlic, and salt in a food processor. Cover and process until smooth, about 30 seconds.

Arrange the bacon in a single layer on a rimmed baking sheet. Spread the bread cubes in a single layer on a second rimmed baking sheet. Drizzle the olive oil over the bread cubes, sprinkle with salt, and, using clean hands, toss until evenly coated. Put both baking sheets in the oven. Bake the bread cubes until golden brown, about 10 minutes. Remove the baking sheet with the bread from the oven and set aside to cool. Turn the bacon with a spatula, then continue to bake until crisp, 5 to 10 minutes longer. Remove the baking sheet from the oven and transfer the bacon to paper towels to drain. Let cool completely, then chop it into pieces.

Cut the avocado in half lengthwise around the large pit in the center. Twist the halves in opposite directions to separate them. Using a spoon, scoop out the pit and discard it. Carefully peel the skin off each half, and then cut the avocado into small cubes.

In a large salad bowl, combine the lettuce, tomatoes, bacon, bread cubes, and avocado. Drizzle with the dressing and, using tongs or salad servers, toss to combine. Serve right away.

Chinese Chicken Salad

This salad with shredded chicken has a sweet and tangy dressing—and lots of pizzazz! Swap out any of the veggies that you don't like for ones you do. The dressing also makes a terrific sauce for grilled chicken breasts served with steamed rice.

MAKES 4 SERVINGS

DRESSING

2 tablespoons teriyaki sauce

1 tablespoon canola oil

1 tablespoon mayonnaise

1 tablespoon rice vinegar

1 teaspoon toasted sesame oil

1 teaspoon peeled and grated fresh ginger

SALAD

2 tablespoons sliced almonds

2 small boneless, skinless chicken breast halves

4 cups mixed salad greens or shredded lettuce

½ English cucumber, sliced

1 cup sugar snap peas, trimmed and sliced

⅓ cup drained canned mandarin orange slices

¼ cup canned fried chow mein or rice noodles

To make the dressing, in a small bowl whisk together all of the ingredients until blended.

Put the almonds in a small frying pan. Set the pan over medium heat. Cook, stirring occasionally, until the almonds are lightly browned and smell toasty, 4 to 5 minutes. Transfer to a bowl and let cool completely.

Put the chicken breasts in a small saucepan, add just enough water to cover, and cover with the lid. Set the pan over medium heat and bring to a simmer. Reduce the heat to low and cook until the chicken is opaque when cut into with a knife, 10 to 15 minutes. Using tongs, transfer the chicken to a plate and let cool. When the chicken is cool enough to handle, use your fingers to shred the chicken into bite-sized pieces. Set aside.

In a large serving bowl, combine the salad greens, cucumber, and sugar snap peas. Using tongs or salad servers, toss gently to combine. Scatter the chicken over the top and sprinkle with the almonds and orange slices. Drizzle the dressing over the top and gently toss to combine. Divide the salad among 4 plates, sprinkle each serving with noodles, and serve.

Chopped Green Salad

You'll love this simple green salad with crunchy cucumber, creamy avocado, and garlic dressing. Add cherry tomatoes, grated carrot, or any of your favorite veggies. To make the salad heartier, top it with sliced hard-boiled eggs.

MAKES 6-8 SERVINGS

DRESSING

¾ cup mayonnaise

1 tablespoon whole milk

2½ teaspoons white wine vinegar

1 clove garlic, minced

½ teaspoon sugar

¼ teaspoon salt

SALAD

2 medium cucumbers

2 ripe avocados

2 or 3 large hearts of romaine lettuce, trimmed and chopped

1 cup garlic croutons

To make the dressing, in a small bowl, whisk together the mayonnaise, milk, vinegar, garlic, sugar, and salt. If the dressing is too thick, add a little water to thin it out. Set aside.

To make the salad, peel the cucumbers, cut them in half lengthwise, and use a spoon to scrape out the seeds. Cut the cucumbers into cubes and add them to a large salad bowl. Cut the avocados in half lengthwise around the large pits in the centers. Twist the halves in opposite directions to separate them. Using a spoon, scoop out the pits and discard them. Carefully peel the skin off of each half, and then cut the avocado into cubes.

Add the lettuce to the cucumbers and, using tongs or salad servers, toss to combine. Scatter the avocados on top and sprinkle with the croutons. You can divide the salad among individual bowls and drizzle the dressing on top, or you can drizzle the dressing over the entire salad, toss gently to mix, and serve from the large bowl. Serve right away.

Chicken Noodle Soup

If you or anyone in your family has the sniffles, make this recipe! Nothing is more comforting when you're sick than homemade chicken noodle soup served with a few crackers. It'll chase away the cold—and make the kitchen smell great, too.

MAKES 4 SERVINGS

2 boneless, skinless chicken breast halves

6 cups low-sodium chicken broth

1 medium carrot, peeled, halved lengthwise, and thinly sliced

1 stalk celery, thinly sliced

1½ teaspoons dried thyme, dill, or parsley

Salt

1½ cups wide egg noodles

Crackers, for serving

Place the chicken breasts in a large saucepan and pour in the chicken broth. Set the pan over medium heat and bring to a boil. Reduce the heat to low and simmer, uncovered, until the chicken is opaque throughout when cut into with a knife, 10 to 15 minutes. Turn off the heat. Using tongs, transfer the chicken breasts to a plate and set aside to cool. Leave the pan of broth on the stovetop.

Add the carrot, celery, and thyme into the pan with the broth. Turn on the heat to medium and bring the broth to a gentle simmer. Cook the vegetables, stirring occasionally, until tender, about 10 minutes. Taste the broth (careful, it's hot!) and season with salt if you think it needs some.

When the chicken is cool enough to handle, use your fingers to shred it into bite-sized pieces. Add the shredded chicken to the simmering broth along with the egg noodles. Cook until the noodles are tender but not mushy, about 5 minutes.

Ladle the soup into bowls and serve right away with crackers.

Corn & Potato Chowder

Chunky, creamy chowder (a hearty kind of soup) is perfect for lunch or a dinner. In the summer, use fresh corn since it's in season, but in the winter, use frozen corn kernels. Serve in mugs with thick slices of warm sourdough bread alongside, perfect for dunking.

MAKES 6-8 SERVINGS

2 slices uncooked bacon, finely chopped

½ yellow onion, chopped

1 carrot, peeled and chopped

2 stalks celery, chopped

5 small red new potatoes, peeled and cut into 1-inch pieces

4 cups low-sodium chicken broth

2 cups fresh or frozen corn kernels

1 cup heavy cream

Salt and ground black pepper

Put the bacon in a large saucepan. Set the pan over medium heat and cook the bacon, stirring occasionally, until crisp, about 8 minutes. Transfer to paper towels with a slotted spoon.

Add the onion, carrot, and celery to the pan and cook, stirring occasionally, until tender. Add the potatoes and chicken broth and stir well. Raise the heat to high and bring to a boil, and then reduce the heat to medium-low and simmer, uncovered, until the potatoes are tender, about 20 minutes.

Add the reserved bacon, the corn, and the cream and cook until the corn is tender and the soup is warmed through, about 5 minutes. Taste the chowder (careful, it's hot!) and season with salt and pepper.

Ladle the chowder into soup mugs or bowls and serve right away.

Toppings galore

Sour cream, salsa, and/or chopped cherry tomatoes also make great toppings for this hearty chili.

Turkey Chili

A big steaming bowl of this chili is great on a rainy day. Serve it topped with shredded cheese and a dollop of sour cream, and a slice of warm cornbread alongside. Spoon leftovers over a hot baked potato!

MAKES 6-8 SERVINGS

1 red or green bell pepper

2 tablespoons olive oil

1 small yellow onion, chopped

2 pounds ground dark-meat turkey

3 cloves garlic, minced

¼ cup mild chili powder

Salt and ground black pepper

One 14½-ounce can crushed tomatoes

Two 15-ounce cans kidney beans or pinto beans, rinsed and drained

1 cup low-sodium chicken broth

Shredded cheese, for serving

Sliced green onions, for serving

Cut the bell pepper in half lengthwise. Using a paring knife, remove the stem, seedy core, and ribs and discard. Cut into thin strips. A few at a time, gather the strips into a bundle and cut them crosswise to form small cubes.

Put the olive oil in a large, heavy pot. Set the pot over medium-high heat. Add the bell pepper and onion and cook, stirring occasionally, until softened, about 7 minutes. Add the ground turkey and cook, breaking up clumps with a wooden spoon, until the meat begins to brown, 7 to 8 minutes. Add the garlic, chili powder, ½ teaspoon salt, and ¼ teaspoon pepper and cook, stirring often, for 1 minute. Add the tomatoes, beans, and chicken broth. Bring to a simmer, and then reduce the heat to medium-low. Cook, uncovered and stirring occasionally, until the chili is nice and thick, 8 to 10 minutes. Taste the chili (careful, it's hot!) and adjust the seasoning with salt and pepper.

Ladle the chili into bowls and serve right away with the cheese and green onions.

Creamy Tomato Soup with Cheese Toasts

Tomato-rific soup and warm, melty cheese toasts (open-faced grilled cheese sandwiches) are an awesome pair. If you're taking the soup on the go, crackers and sliced cheese are a great easy-to-pack alternative.

MAKES 6 SERVINGS

SOUP

2 tablespoons unsalted butter

1 tablespoon olive oil

1 small yellow onion, coarsely chopped

2 cloves garlic, minced

One 28-ounce can diced tomatoes

4 cups low-sodium chicken or vegetable broth

½ cup heavy cream

½ teaspoon salt

¼ teaspoon ground black pepper (optional)

CHEESE TOASTS

8 to 12 slices baguette, cut on the diagonal

½ cup shredded Cheddar or Monterey jack cheese

To make the soup, put the butter and oil in a large saucepan. Set the pan over medium heat. When the butter is melted, add the onion and cook, stirring often, until tender and translucent, about 7 minutes. Add the garlic and cook, stirring often, for 2 minutes longer. Add the tomatoes and their juices and the chicken broth. Raise the heat to high and bring to a boil, and then reduce the heat to medium-low and simmer, stirring occasionally, for 20 minutes.

Remove the saucepan from the heat and let the tomato mixture cool slightly. Using an immersion blender, purée the soup in the saucepan until smooth. (If you're using a regular blender, let the soup cool until lukewarm. Working in batches, transfer the soup to the blender and purée until smooth. Pour each batch into a large bowl, and when all of the soup is puréed, pour it back into the saucepan.)

Return the saucepan to medium-low heat and stir in the cream, salt, and pepper, if using. Heat the soup, stirring occasionally, until steaming. Turn off the heat and cover to keep warm.

To make the cheese toasts, preheat the broiler. Place the baguette slices in a single layer on a baking sheet and top them with the cheese, dividing it evenly. Broil the toasts until the cheese is melted, 1 to 2 minutes. Remove the baking sheet from the oven.

Ladle the soup into bowls and serve right away with the cheese toasts.

Main Dishes

Put a star on it

For extra fun, cut the cheese slices into stars with a star-shaped cookie cutter!

Turkey Sliders with Aioli

Keep these cute little burgers simple or jazz them up with toppings like sliced avocado or cooked bacon. You can swap Swiss cheese, Monterey jack, or provolone for the Cheddar. And if aioli isn't your thing, use plain mayo.

MAKES 8 SLIDERS

AIOLI

½ cup mayonnaise

2 cloves garlic, minced

¼ teaspoon coarse sea salt

SLIDERS

1 pound ground dark-meat turkey

1 tablespoon ketchup

2 teaspoons Dijon mustard

¼ teaspoon salt

¼ teaspoon ground black pepper

8 slices Cheddar cheese

8 slider buns or dinner rolls, split horizontally

8 small romaine lettuce leaves

8 thin slices tomato

To make the aioli, in a small bowl, whisk the mayonnaise, garlic, and salt until blended. Cover with plastic wrap and refrigerate until you're ready to assemble the sliders.

To make the sliders, in a medium bowl, combine the ground turkey, ketchup, mustard, salt, and pepper. Using clean hands, mix until well combined, and then divide the mixture into 8 equal pieces. Shape each piece into a patty.

Grease a large grill pan or frying pan with cooking spray. Set the pan over medium-high heat. Let the pan heat for 3 minutes, and then carefully add the patties in a single layer. Cook until browned on the bottoms, about 5 minutes. Using a wide metal spatula, flip the patties. Place a slice of cheese on each patty and cook until the cheese is melted and the patties are cooked to your liking, about 5 minutes longer. Using the spatula, transfer the patties to a plate. Place the rolls cut side down in the pan and toast until lightly browned, 1 to 4 minutes.

Spread the toasted sides of the bottom halves of the rolls with aioli. Top each with a lettuce leaf and a slice of tomato, and then top with a patty, cheese side up. Cover with the top halves of the rolls and serve right away.

Fish Sticks & Homemade Tartar Sauce

Homemade fish sticks are our favorites and beat out store-bought any day. Making tartar sauce is easy! Just stir together the mayo, pickles, parsley, capers, and lemon juice in a small bowl.

MAKES 4 SERVINGS

TARTAR SAUCE

½ cup mayonnaise

¼ cup finely chopped bread-and-butter pickles

1 tablespoon finely chopped fresh flat-leaf parsley

2 teaspoons drained capers, chopped

1 teaspoon fresh lemon juice

FISH STICKS

1½ pounds thick skinless cod or tilapia fillets

1 teaspoon salt

½ cup all-purpose flour

2 large eggs, beaten

1 cup plain dried bread crumbs or panko

3 tablespoons canola oil

Preheat the oven to 450°F. Prepare the tartar sauce (see Note, above), cover, and set aside.

To make the fish sticks, cut the fish fillets into strips about 1 inch wide and 3 to 4 inches long. Sprinkle the strips all over with the salt.

Put the flour, eggs, and bread crumbs in 3 separate shallow bowls or baking dishes. Line up the bowls in that order from left to right and place a large plate to the right of the bread crumbs.

Coat each piece of fish on all sides with flour and tap off the excess. Dip the flour-coated fish into the eggs, turn to coat, and allow the excess to drip off. Finally, dip the fish into the bread crumbs and turn to coat all sides, pressing so that the bread crumbs stick. Set the breaded fish on the plate.

Pour the canola oil onto a large rimmed baking sheet and use a pastry brush to coat the entire surface. Place the baking sheet in the oven and allow it to heat for 5 minutes. Remove the baking sheet from the oven. Carefully place the breaded fish sticks in a single layer on the hot baking sheet, making sure they don't touch. Bake, turning the fish sticks halfway through with a metal spatula, until crisp and golden, about 12 minutes.

Remove the baking sheet from the oven and transfer the fish sticks to a platter. Serve warm, with the tartar sauce for dipping.

Turkey Club Sandwiches

Like all classic club sandwiches, this one is a double-decker and makes a hefty sandwich that's good to share! For a fun presentation, cut each sandwich into quarters and skewer each section with a frilly toothpick!

MAKES 2 SANDWICHES

3 slices thick-cut bacon

6 slices whole-wheat or multigrain sandwich bread

½ ripe avocado

Mayonnaise

4 slices smoked turkey

2 large lettuce leaves

4 thin slices tomato

Lay the bacon slices in a single layer in a medium frying pan. Set the pan over medium heat and fry the bacon, turning the slices once, until golden and crisp, about 5 minutes. Transfer the bacon to a paper towel–lined plate to drain.

Toast the bread slices in a toaster until golden.

If the avocado half contains the pit, use a spoon to scoop out the pit and discard. Carefully peel off the skin, and then use a dinner knife to cut the avocado into thin slices.

Spread a thin layer of mayonnaise on 1 side of 2 of the toasted bread slices. Arrange the avocado slices on the mayo-coated sides of the bread, dividing them evenly, and then arrange 2 slices of turkey on each. Spread more mayonnaise on each side of another 2 slices of toasted bread and place on top of the turkey. Top each with a lettuce leaf, breaking it to fit on the bread, followed by tomato slices. Break the bacon slices in half and arrange 3 pieces of bacon in a single layer over the tomatoes on each sandwich. Spread more mayonnaise on 1 side of the remaining 2 toasted bread slices. Place each slice, mayo-side down, on top of the bacon and press down gently.

Cut the sandwiches in half on the diagonal. Serve right away.

Spiced Beef Tacos

Plan a fun-filled fiesta and offer up Guacamole & Star Chips (page 26) and these awesomely good tacos. Instead of assembling the tacos yourself, set the toppings out in bowls and let everyone build their own. And make sure to have lots of napkins on hand!

MAKES 6 TACOS

1 tablespoon canola oil

¼ cup chopped yellow onion

1 clove garlic, minced

1 pound ground beef

1 teaspoon ground cumin

2 teaspoons sweet paprika

2 teaspoons mild chili powder

1 teaspoon salt

¼ teaspoon ground black pepper

¼ cup water

Six 8-inch flour or whole-wheat tortillas

1 ripe avocado

1 heaping cup shredded lettuce

2 plum tomatoes, chopped

½ cup shredded Cheddar cheese

Preheat the oven to 300°F.

Put the canola oil in a large frying pan or sauté pan. Set the pan over medium heat. Add the onion and garlic and cook, stirring occasionally, until softened, about 7 minutes. Add the ground beef and cook, breaking up clumps with a wooden spoon, until browned, 8 to 10 minutes. Spoon off and discard all but 1 tablespoon of the fat in the pan. Add the cumin, paprika, chili powder, salt, and pepper to the beef and stir until combined. Add the water and bring to a simmer, and then reduce the heat to low, cover partially, and cook, stirring occasionally, until most of the water is gone, about 10 minutes. Remove from the heat and cover the pan to keep warm.

Stack the tortillas and wrap them in aluminum foil. Place in the oven to warm for 5 minutes.

While the tortillas are warming, cut the avocado in half lengthwise around the large pit in the center. Twist the halves in opposite directions to separate them. Using a spoon, scoop out the pit and discard it. Carefully peel the skin off each half, and then cut the avocado into small cubes.

Remove the tortillas from the oven and unwrap them. Place 1 tortilla on each of 6 plates. Spoon on the beef filling, dividing it evenly. Sprinkle each with an equal amount of lettuce, tomatoes, avocado, and cheese. Fold each tortilla in half and serve right away.

Veggie tacos

Try swapping out the beef with 2 cans of drained pinto or black beans; just simmer them with the spices and use like beef!

Homemade Pizza

Nothing is more fun than having your best friends over for a homemade pizza party. And the best part is you can each make your dream pizza! You can serve your pizzas with lemonade and a Chopped Green Salad (page 47) for a full meal.

MAKES **12** SMALL PIZZAS

DOUGH

8 cups all-purpose flour

2 packages instant or rapid-rise yeast (4½ teaspoons total)

1 teaspoon salt

3 cups lukewarm water

2 tablespoons olive oil, plus more for oiling the bowl

Cornmeal or semolina for dusting the baking sheets

TOMATO SAUCE

1 tablespoon olive oil

¼ yellow onion, finely chopped

1 clove garlic, minced

One 28-ounce can diced tomatoes, drained

1 tablespoon tomato paste

½ teaspoon dried oregano or basil

Salt and ground black pepper

To make the dough, in the bowl of a stand mixer, whisk together the flour, yeast, and salt. Fit the mixer with the dough hook, add the water and olive oil, and mix on medium speed until a dough forms and pulls cleanly away from the sides of the bowl, about 8 minutes.

Lightly grease a large bowl with olive oil, place the dough in the bowl, and turn the dough over. Cover with plastic wrap and let rise in a warm place until doubled in bulk, about 45 minutes, or in the refrigerator for up to 12 hours.

To make the tomato sauce, put the olive oil in a large saucepan. Set the pan over medium heat. Add the onion and cook, stirring occasionally, until tender and translucent, about 10 minutes. Add the garlic and cook, stirring constantly, for 1 minute longer. Add the tomatoes, tomato paste, and oregano, stirring to combine. Raise the heat to medium-high and cook, stirring occasionally and breaking up the tomatoes with a wooden spoon, until the sauce is thick, 10 to 15 minutes. Taste the sauce (careful, it's hot!) and season with salt and pepper. Let cool and transfer to a bowl.

Position a rack in the lower third of the oven and preheat the oven to 425°F. Lightly sprinkle 2 rimmed baking sheets with cornmeal. (If the dough has risen in the refrigerator, remove the bowl from the refrigerator and let the dough come to room temperature for about 1 hour before continuing.) Turn out the dough onto a floured work surface and, using a knife, divide into 12 equal pieces.

Pizza art

Use your favorite toppings to make pretty designs, like flowers, faces, or fun patterns to create a unique piece of food art.

TOPPING IDEAS

Shredded mozzarella cheese

Sliced mushrooms

Sliced cooked Italian sausage

Sliced pepperoni

Halved cherry tomatoes

Sliced pitted olives

Sliced zucchini

Roasted red bell pepper slices

Cooked broccoli florets

Set out your favorite toppings in separate bowls, along with the tomato sauce, and let the party begin! Give each person a piece of dough. Gently press and stretch the dough into a circle about 7 inches in diameter. (Don't work the dough too much or it won't hold its shape.) Spread the round with a thin layer of tomato sauce, sprinkle with some cheese, and add the toppings of your choice.

Place 2 pizza rounds on each prepared baking sheet and bake one sheet at a time until the crust is golden and the cheese is bubbly, 12 to 15 minutes. Remove the baking sheet from the oven. Repeat to bake the remaining pizza rounds.

Let the pizzas cool for a few minutes on the baking sheet, and then use a wide metal spatula to transfer them to a cutting board. Cut each one into quarters and serve each guest his or her own creation.

Pizza Party Game Plan

Before the party, make the pizza dough, cook the tomato sauce, and divide the dough into 12 portions. Then when guests show up, set out as many different types of toppings as you like, put the tomato sauce in a bowl, and give each person a piece of dough to shape and top. You'll have to bake the pizzas two at a time, but serve them hot out of the oven—and encourage sharing!

Rosemary Roast Chicken

The next time you want to make a really special meal for your family, pull out this recipe! This juicy roasted chicken is great served with Creamiest Mashed Potatoes (page 106) and Sautéed Green Beans with Almonds (page 105).

MAKES 4-6 SERVINGS

Juice of 1 lemon

¼ cup olive oil

3 tablespoons whole-grain Dijon mustard

2 tablespoons chopped fresh rosemary leaves

¼ teaspoon salt

Pinch of ground black pepper

2 bone-in chicken breast halves

2 chicken drumsticks

2 bone-in chicken thighs

In a large glass or ceramic baking dish, stir together the lemon juice, olive oil, mustard, rosemary, salt, and pepper. Add the chicken pieces and use tongs to turn and coat them with the marinade. Cover the baking dish with plastic wrap and refrigerate for at least 1 hour or up to overnight, turning the chicken pieces once.

Remove the baking dish from the refrigerator and uncover. If the chicken pieces are skin side down, turn them skin side up. Let the chicken stand at room temperature for 30 minutes. After 15 minutes, preheat the oven to 400°F.

Put the baking dish in the oven and roast the chicken until the skin is browned, about 50 minutes. Remove the dish from the oven. To test if the chicken is done, slide the tip of a paring knife into and out of the thickest part of a drumstick. The juices should run clear; if they are pink, return the chicken to the oven, cook for 5 to 10 minutes longer, and then test again.

Using tongs, transfer the chicken pieces to a platter. Spoon some of the cooking juices over the top and serve right away.

Fish Tacos with Slaw

In addition to the tangy slaw, you can top these yummy tacos with a squeeze of lime juice, a dollop of sour cream, a sprinkle of fresh chopped cilantro, or spoonfuls of salsa. Or, if you like, add them all!

MAKES 6 SERVINGS

SLAW

4 cups finely shredded green and purple cabbage

3 tablespoons chopped fresh cilantro

¼ cup chopped green onion (optional)

¼ cup fresh lime juice

2 teaspoons sugar

Salt

12 corn tortillas

1 pound skinless, boneless firm white fish fillets, such as cod or snapper

Canola oil for brushing the fish

Ground black pepper

To make the slaw, in a large bowl, combine the cabbage, cilantro, green onion (if using), lime juice, sugar, and ¼ teaspoon salt and mix well. Let stand at room temperature for 20 minutes, and then taste and add more salt if you like. Cover the bowl with plastic wrap and refrigerate until you're ready to assemble the tacos.

Ask an adult to help you prepare a medium-high fire in a gas or charcoal grill or have ready a stovetop grill pan. Stack the tortillas and wrap them in aluminum foil.

Lightly brush the fish on both sides with canola oil and season with salt and pepper. If using a stovetop grill pan, preheat it over medium-high heat on the stovetop; brush the grill pan with oil. If using the grill, clean and oil the grill grate. Place the fish fillets on the grill grate or grill pan. Cook, turning once with a wide metal spatula, until browned on both sides and the flesh is opaque throughout, 3 to 4 minutes on each side. Meanwhile, place the foil-wrapped tortillas on the grill grate or grill pan and warm them, turning the packet once or twice, for about 5 minutes. Transfer the fish to a plate and divide the fillets into 12 equal pieces, discarding any bones.

Unwrap the tortillas. To assemble each serving, place 2 warm tortillas on a plate, top each one with a piece of fish, and add some slaw. Serve the tacos right away as you assemble each serving.

Baked Chicken Parmesan

Crisp, crunchy chicken topped with tangy tomato sauce and gooey mozzarella cheese is an Italian-American favorite. To make Baked Eggplant Parmesan, a vegetarian version that's every bit as yummy, see the variation at the end of this recipe. *Mangia!*

MAKES 12 SERVINGS

3 tablespoons olive oil, plus more for greasing the baking dish

6 small boneless, skinless chicken breast halves

Salt

1 cup all-purpose flour

3 large eggs, beaten

1½ cups plain dried bread crumbs

½ cup grated Parmesan cheese

1 pound fresh mozzarella cheese, cut into thin slices

3 cups homemade or store-bought marinara sauce

Pour the olive oil onto a rimmed baking sheet and use a pastry brush to coat the entire surface. Place 1 chicken breast half inside a zipper-lock freezer bag and pound with a meat pounder until it is ½ inch thick. Transfer to a large plate and repeat with the remaining chicken breast halves. Season the chicken breasts on both sides with salt.

Preheat the oven to 400°F. Put the flour, eggs, and bread crumbs in 3 separate shallow bowls or baking dishes. Line up the bowls in that order from left to right. Stir the Parmesan into the bread crumbs.

One at a time, coat the chicken breasts on both sides with flour and tap off the excess. Dip the flour-coated chicken into the eggs, turn to coat, and allow the excess to drip off. Finally, dip the breasts into the bread crumbs and turn to coat both sides, pressing so that the bread crumbs stick. Place on the prepared baking sheet in a single layer.

Bake for 15 minutes. Remove the baking sheet from the oven. Using a wide metal spatula, carefully turn the chicken breasts. Continue to bake until golden on both sides, about 15 minutes longer. Remove the baking sheet from the oven and set aside. Leave the oven on.

Italian feast

Serve this yummy cheesy dish with a big pile of buttered spaghetti or sautéed spinach or both!

Lightly grease a 9-by-13-inch baking dish with olive oil. Pour in 2 cups of marinara sauce and spread it into an even layer. Use a spatula to arrange the warm chicken breasts in the baking dish, overlapping them slightly, and pour the remaining 1 cup of marinara sauce evenly over the top, then lay the mozzarella slices on top. Bake until the cheese is melted and the sauce is bubbling, about 20 minutes.

Remove the baking dish from the oven. Let cool for 10 minutes and serve.

Variation: Eggplant Parmesan

Pour 3 tablespoons of olive oil onto each of 2 rimmed baking sheets and use a pastry brush to coat the entire surfaces. Trim 2 small globe eggplants (1½ pounds total) and slice them into ½-inch-thick rounds. Sprinkle both sides of the slices with salt and set aside for 20 minutes (the salt will help remove some of the bitterness from the eggplant). Pat the slices dry with paper towels. Follow the recipe for Baked Chicken Parmesan, using the eggplant slices in place of the chicken breasts, arranging them in a single layer on the prepared baking sheets. When arranging the baked eggplant in the prepared baking dish, tuck the mozzarella between the eggplant slices instead of placing it on top. Increase the amount of marinara to 4 cups. Bake as directed.

Spaghetti & Meatballs

A mound of spaghetti topped with turkey meatballs and cheese? Yes, please! The meatballs are also delish stuffed into crusty rolls and topped with tomato sauce and Parmesan cheese.

MAKES **4-6** SERVINGS

SAUCE

2 tablespoons olive oil

½ yellow onion, chopped

1 clove garlic, minced

One 15-ounce can tomato purée

One 14½-ounce can diced tomatoes with juices

One 6-ounce can tomato paste

2 tablespoons dried oregano

Salt and ground black pepper

To make the sauce, pour the olive oil into a large saucepan. Set the pan over medium heat. Add the onion and garlic and cook, stirring occasionally, until the onion is soft, about 5 minutes. Add the tomato purée, diced tomatoes and their juices, tomato paste, and oregano and stir to combine. Bring to a simmer, and then reduce the heat to medium-low and cook, stirring occasionally, until thickened, about 20 minutes. Season to taste with salt and pepper. Remove the pan from the heat, cover, and set aside.

~ *Continued on page 87* ~

Super sauce

This yummy spaghetti sauce is loaded with flavor. You can double it and freeze half for later, too!

~ Continued from page 84 ~

MEATBALLS

2 tablespoons olive oil

1½ pounds ground dark-meat turkey

1 cup fresh bread crumbs

½ cup grated Parmesan cheese

2 large eggs

1 tablespoon dried oregano

Salt and ground black pepper

1 pound spaghetti

Grated Parmesan cheese for serving

To make the meatballs, preheat the oven to 450°F. Pour the olive oil onto a rimmed baking sheet and use a pastry brush to coat the entire surface.

In a large bowl, combine the ground turkey, bread crumbs, Parmesan, eggs, and oregano. Season with salt and pepper. Using clean hands, mix until well combined. Scoop out tablespoon-sized portions of the turkey mixture, rolling each one between your palms to form a small ball.

Place the meatballs in a single layer on the baking sheet, making sure they don't touch. Bake until the meatballs are browned and cooked through, about 15 minutes.

Remove the baking sheet from the oven and transfer the meatballs to the pan of tomato sauce. Set the pan over low heat and cook, stirring occasionally and gently, about 20 minutes.

While the meatballs simmer, fill a large pot three-fourths full of water. Set the pot over high heat and bring the water to a boil. Add 1 tablespoon salt and the spaghetti, stir well, and cook according to the package directions until al dente (tender but firm at the center). Drain the spaghetti in a colander set in the sink and divide among warmed serving bowls. Ladle sauce and meatballs over the top, sprinkle with Parmesan, and serve right away.

Teriyaki Chicken & Veggies

This stir-fry is quick and easy to cook, and the different-colored veggies make it pretty, too. There's lots of sweet-and-salty sauce in this dish, so make sure to serve it with steamed rice for soaking up the yumminess!

MAKES 4 SERVINGS

TERIYAKI SAUCE

⅓ cup low-sodium chicken broth

⅓ cup low-sodium soy sauce

1 tablespoon packed light brown sugar

2 teaspoons cornstarch

1 large clove garlic, smashed

½ red bell pepper

1 tablespoon olive oil

8 baby carrots, cut lengthwise into sticks

1 heaping cup sliced mushrooms

1 cup sugar snap peas or snow peas, trimmed and cut in half

2 boneless, skinless chicken breast halves, cut crosswise into ¼-inch strips

Steamed jasmine rice for serving

To make the sauce, put the chicken broth, soy sauce, brown sugar, cornstarch, and garlic in a food processor. Cover and process until smooth, about 30 seconds.

Using a paring knife, remove the stem, seedy core, and whitish ribs and discard. Cut the pepper lengthwise into thin strips.

Put the olive oil in a large frying pan. Set the pan over medium heat. Heat the oil for 1 minute, and then add the carrots and the bell pepper strips. Stir to coat with oil, cover, and cook, stirring occasionally, until the veggies are crisp-tender, about 5 minutes. Stir in the mushrooms and cook until they're nearly tender, about 3 minutes. Add the sugar snap peas and the chicken and cook, stirring often, until the chicken is no longer pink, about 5 minutes.

Whisk the sauce, then pour it into the pan and cook, stirring constantly, until the sauce is simmering and slightly thickened, 1 to 2 minutes.

Spoon rice onto individual plates, top with the stir-fry and some sauce, and serve right away.

Hawaiian Chicken Kebabs

Food on a stick is so much fun to cook and to eat! With chunks of pineapple, cubes of chicken, and a soy-ginger sauce, these kebabs are loaded with yummy sweet and savory flavors. Serve them with steamed rice and sugar snap peas.

MAKES 6-8 SERVINGS

½ cup pineapple juice

3 tablespoons olive oil, plus more for brushing the kebabs

2 tablespoons soy sauce

2 tablespoons packed light brown sugar

1 tablespoon peeled and grated fresh ginger

1 clove garlic, minced

3 boneless, skinless chicken breast halves (about 1½ pounds total), cut into 1½-inch cubes

2 cups fresh pineapple, cut into 1-inch chunks

Have ready 12 to 16 skewers. (If you're using wooden skewers, soak them in water to cover for at least 15 minutes, and then drain.) Ask an adult to help you prepare a medium fire in a gas or charcoal grill or have ready a stovetop grill pan.

In a small bowl, combine the pineapple juice, olive oil, soy sauce, sugar, ginger, and garlic. Stir until the sugar dissolves. This is the basting sauce.

Thread 2 or 3 chicken pieces alternately with 2 or 3 pineapple chunks onto each skewer. Brush the kebabs lightly with olive oil, and then brush them liberally with some of the basting sauce.

If using a stovetop grill pan, preheat it over medium-high heat on the stovetop; brush the grill pan with oil. If using the grill, clean and oil the grill grate.

Place the kebabs on the grate or grill pan. Cook, brushing them often with basting sauce and turning with tongs as needed, until lightly browned on all sides and the chicken is opaque throughout when cut into with a knife, 7 to 10 minutes. If you have any basting sauce left over, discard it.

Transfer the kebabs to a platter and serve right away.

Ham, Cheese & Roasted Red Pepper Panini

A panini is a sandwich that's pressed during cooking so that the bread becomes nice and crisp and the cheese gets extra gooey. For the ultimate grilled cheese sandwich, skip the roasted pepper and ham and use two or three different types of cheese.

MAKES 2 PANINI

4 slices sourdough bread

8 slices provolone, Monterey jack, or Swiss cheese

1 jarred roasted red pepper, drained and finely chopped

4 slices Black Forest ham or honey ham

2 tablespoons unsalted butter, at room temperature

Lay 2 of the bread slices on a clean work surface and top each with 2 slices of cheese, half of the chopped roasted pepper, 2 slices of ham, and another 2 slices of cheese. Top each sandwich with 1 of the remaining bread slices. Spread the butter on the outside of the sandwiches, dividing it evenly among the sides.

Place a griddle or large nonstick frying pan over medium heat and let it heat for 3 minutes. Put the panini on the griddle and cook, turning once, until golden brown on both sides, 2 to 3 minutes per side. As the panini cook, use a wide metal spatula to gently press them down once or twice on each side.

Using the spatula, transfer the panini to a cutting board. Let cool for 1 to 2 minutes to let the cheese set slightly. Cut each panini in half diagonally. Serve right away.

Sandwich stuffings

Create your favorite panini with toppings you love, like smoked turkey, chopped tomatoes, or a smear of pesto.

Sesame Noodles with Peanut Sauce

Here, noodles are tossed with a rich, peanutty sauce and crisp, colorful veggies. Broccoli florets, sugar snap peas, or chopped asparagus are awesome substitutes for the carrots or snow peas. Or add 2 cups shredded cooked chicken along with the cooked veggies.

MAKES 5 SERVINGS

2 carrots

Salt

¼ pound snow peas, trimmed

½ pound spaghetti, broken in half

1 teaspoon toasted sesame oil

3½ tablespoons fresh lime juice

3 tablespoons soy sauce

2½ tablespoons creamy peanut butter

2 teaspoons well-stirred tahini

1½ teaspoons Asian chile paste, such as sambal oelek (optional)

¼ cup chopped roasted peanuts

Peel the carrots and slice them diagonally into ⅛-inch-thick ovals. Cut each oval lengthwise into matchsticks.

Fill a large pot three-fourths full of water. Set the pot over high heat and bring the water to a boil. Add 2 teaspoons salt and the snow peas and cook just until the peas are crisp-tender, about 1 minute. Using a slotted spoon, transfer the peas to a medium bowl. Add the carrot matchsticks to the pot and cook until just crisp-tender, about 2 minutes. Transfer to the bowl with snow peas and set aside. Add the spaghetti to the boiling water and cook according to package directions until al dente (tender but still firm at the center). Reserve ¼ cup of the cooking water, and then drain noodles in a colander set in the sink. Return the noodles to the pot, add the sesame oil, and toss with tongs until evenly coated.

In a small bowl, whisk together the lime juice, soy sauce, peanut butter, tahini, chile paste (if using), and reserved pasta water until blended. Add the mixture to the pasta along with the vegetables and toss with tongs until evenly coated and the veggies are evenly distributed.

Transfer the noodles to a serving bowl, sprinkle with the chopped peanuts, and serve right away.

Baked Penne with Spinach & Cheese

This baked pasta is a hearty, super-tasty vegetarian dish. If you're a meat lover, you won't even notice that it's meat-free! Cheesy Garlic Bread (page 102) is perfect to serve alongside.

MAKES 6 SERVINGS

1 tablespoon unsalted butter, plus more for greasing the baking dish

Salt

¾ pound penne pasta

One 10-ounce container fresh baby spinach

1 cup crumbled feta cheese

1 cup sour cream

½ cup plain whole-milk yogurt

½ cup shredded mozzarella or grated Parmesan cheese

Preheat the oven to 375°F. Butter a 9-by-13-inch baking dish.

Fill a large pot three-fourths full of water. Set the pot over high heat and bring the water to a boil. Add 1 tablespoon salt and the pasta, stir well, and cook the pasta according to the package directions until al dente (tender but still firm at the center). Drain in a colander set in the sink, transfer the pasta to a bowl, and set aside. Return the colander to the sink.

Add the butter to a large frying pan. Set the pan over medium heat. When the butter has melted, add the spinach in 2 or 3 batches, stirring until slightly wilted before adding the next batch. Stir in a pinch of salt and cook until the spinach is completely wilted. Drain the spinach in the colander and press down on it with a rubber spatula to remove as much liquid as possible. Transfer the spinach to a cutting board and finely chop.

In a large bowl, stir the feta, sour cream, yogurt, and spinach until well combined. Add the pasta and stir until evenly coated. Pour the mixture into the prepared baking dish, spread into an even layer, and sprinkle the mozzarella evenly over the top. Bake until hot and bubbly, about 30 minutes.

Remove the baking dish from the oven. Serve right away.

Side Dishes

Sweet Potato Chips

Did you know you can make potato chips at home in your oven? And it's super easy! This version uses sweet potatoes, but you can use the same method with russet potatoes or try a variety of root vegetables.

MAKES 2 SERVINGS

1 small sweet potato (about ¼ pound), peeled

1 tablespoon olive oil

Salt

Preheat the oven to 400°F. Line a baking sheet with parchment paper.

Using the thinnest slicing disk on a food processor or a sharp knife and a very steady hand, slice the sweet potato crosswise into very thin ⅛-inch rounds. Put the slices in a large bowl and drizzle with the olive oil. Using your hands, gently toss the slices very gently until evenly coated.

Lay the sweet potato slices in a single layer, overlapping them as little as possible, on the prepared baking sheet. Use a pastry brush to spread the oil remaining in the bowl on any uncoated slices. Bake for 10 minutes. Remove the baking sheet from the oven and, using a wide metal spatula, turn over all of the slices. Sprinkle with ¼ teaspoon salt and continue to bake until the slices are dry and some are lightly browned, about 10 minutes longer. Check often during the last few minutes of baking.

Remove the baking sheet from the oven and slide the chips into a serving bowl. Sprinkle with a little more salt and serve warm.

Cheesy Garlic Bread

Who can resist buttery garlic bread with lots of melted cheese? It's the perfect companion to any soup or pasta dish, and it's also great on its own as a savory after-school or movie-night snack.

MAKES 8 SERVINGS

½ cup unsalted butter

3 large cloves garlic, minced

1 teaspoon minced fresh flat-leaf parsley (optional)

1 loaf Italian bread, cut in half horizontally

1½ cups shredded mozzarella cheese or grated Parmesan cheese

Preheat the oven to 450°F.

In a small frying pan, combine the butter and garlic. Set the pan over medium heat. Cook, stirring constantly, until the butter is completely melted. Stir in the parsley (if using) and remove the pan from the heat.

Place the bread halves cut sides up on a rimmed baking sheet. Using a pastry brush, brush the butter mixture evenly on the cut sides of the bread. Top with the cheese, dividing it evenly between the halves. Bake until the cheese is melted and the edges are toasted and golden brown, 5 to 7 minutes.

Remove the baking sheet from the oven. Let the bread cool slightly, and then transfer to a cutting board. Cut the bread crosswise into thick slices and serve right away.

Sautéed Green Beans with Almonds

These green beans get all dressed up with a few simple additions: sweet-tart balsamic vinegar, creamy butter, and toasty almonds. This dish is the perfect addition to a special dinner or holiday meal, but it's also easy enough to make on a school night!

MAKES 4-6 SERVINGS

2 tablespoons sliced almonds

Salt

1 pound thin green beans, trimmed and cut into 1-inch lengths

1 tablespoon unsalted butter

2 teaspoons balsamic vinegar

Ground black pepper

Put the almonds in a small frying pan. Set the pan over medium heat. Cook, stirring occasionally, until the almonds are lightly browned and smell toasty, 4 to 5 minutes. Transfer to a bowl and let cool completely.

Fill a large saucepan half full with water. Set the pan over high heat and bring the water to a boil. Add 1 teaspoon salt and the beans and boil until the beans are bright green and just tender, 3 to 5 minutes. Drain the beans in a colander set in the sink and rinse under cold running water. Drain well.

Add the butter to a large frying pan. Set the pan over low heat. When the butter is melted, add the green beans and the vinegar. Raise the heat to medium and cook, tossing with tongs, until the beans are heated through, about 1 minute. Taste the beans (careful, they're hot!) and season with salt and pepper. Transfer to a bowl or platter, sprinkle with the almonds, and serve right away.

Creamiest Mashed Potatoes

Have you ever met anyone who doesn't love a big, pillowy mound of creamy mashed potatoes? For a super-yummy, cheesy twist, stir in ½ cup grated Cheddar or Monterey jack along with the milk mixture.

MAKES 6-8 SERVINGS

Salt

2 pounds Yukon gold potatoes, peeled and quartered

½ cup whole milk

½ cup heavy cream

2 tablespoons unsalted butter, plus 1 tablespoon melted butter

Fill a large saucepan about three-fourths full of water and add 1 tablespoon salt and the potatoes. Set the pan over medium-high heat and bring to a boil. Reduce the heat to medium-low and simmer, uncovered, until you can easily slide a skewer into and out of the potatoes, about 20 minutes. Drain the potatoes in a colander set in the sink.

Transfer the potatoes to a large bowl and mash with a potato masher until very smooth. Cover the bowl with a clean kitchen towel to keep the potatoes warm.

In a small saucepan, combine the milk, cream, and butter. Set the pan over medium heat and bring to a simmer. Gradually add the hot milk mixture to the potatoes while beating with a fork. The potatoes should be smooth and thick. Taste the potatoes, season with salt, and top with the melted butter. Transfer to a bowl and serve right away.

Gold & creamy

Sweet and smooth, Yukon gold potatoes make the best mash, but you can also use russet potatoes in a pinch.

Refried Black Beans

Refried beans are the perfect side to tacos and enchiladas and can be spread onto tostadas or stuffed into burritos. This recipe makes smooth refried beans, but if you like them chunky, purée only two-thirds of the cooked beans.

MAKES 6-8 SERVINGS

1 cup dried black beans

1 small yellow onion, chopped

2 large cloves garlic

1 teaspoon ground cumin

Salt

¼ cup canola oil

½ lime

Cotija cheese or shredded Monterey jack for serving

Pick over the beans, discarding any pebbles and grit. Place the beans in a medium bowl, add water to cover by 4 inches, and soak overnight at room temperature.

Drain the beans in a colander set in the sink, rinse well under running cold water, and transfer to a large saucepan. Add the onion, garlic, cumin, and water to cover by 1 inch. Set the pan over high heat and bring to a gentle boil, using a spoon to skim off any foam that forms on the surface. Reduce the heat to medium-low and simmer for 45 minutes, stirring occasionally. Add 1 teaspoon salt and more water if needed to keep the beans submerged, and continue to cook until the beans are very tender, 15 to 20 minutes longer. Turn off the heat and let the beans cool in their cooking liquid.

Remove about ¼ cup of the cooking liquid, and then drain the beans in a colander set in the sink. Put the beans in a food processor and process until smooth. If the purée is too stiff to move smoothly, add the reserved cooking liquid 1 tablespoon at a time to achieve a very smooth, thick paste.

Put the canola oil in a medium frying pan or sauté pan. Set the pan over medium heat. Add the beans, stir well to incorporate with the oil, and cook, stirring constantly, until the beans sizzle and pull away from the sides of the pan, about 7 minutes. Taste the beans (careful, they're hot!), adjust the seasoning with salt, and squeeze in as much lime juice as you like. Transfer to a bowl, sprinkle with cheese, and serve right away.

Stuffed Baked Potatoes

Potatoes that are baked, hollowed out, stuffed with a cheesy potato mixture, and then baked again make a hearty side dish. You can easily turn them into a meal by adding ¼ cup chopped ham and ¼ cup chopped cooked broccoli florets to the stuffing mixture.

MAKES 4-8 SERVINGS

4 russet baking potatoes, scrubbed

½ cup sour cream

¼ cup whole milk

1¼ cups shredded Cheddar cheese

Salt and ground black pepper

Preheat the oven to 375°F.

Poke the potatoes all over with the tip of a paring knife. Put the potatoes in the oven, directly on the oven rack, and bake until you can easily pierce them with a skewer or dinner fork, about 1 hour.

Remove the potatoes from the oven, but leave the oven on. Set the potatoes aside until they are cool enough to handle.

Cut the potatoes in half lengthwise (careful, the insides may still be hot!). Using a spoon, scoop the potato flesh into a mixing bowl, being careful not to poke through the skin on the bottom and sides. Try to leave a wall of potato flesh about ¼ inch thick, so that the skin won't break when you stuff it. Set the skins, cut sides up, in a baking dish just large enough to hold them in a single layer. Add the sour cream and milk to the potato flesh. Using the spoon, stir and mash the mixture until smooth, and then stir in half of the cheese. Taste and season with salt and pepper.

Using the spoon, scoop the potato mixture into the potato skins, dividing it evenly. Sprinkle with the remaining cheese, dividing it evenly. Bake until the cheese is melted and the potatoes are heated through, about 15 minutes.

Remove the baking dish from the oven and serve right away.

Buttery Peas with Mint

Take simple frozen peas and mix them with butter and mint and you'll experience a taste explosion! This super-easy side dish is great alongside roasted chicken, grilled fish, or a seared steak.

MAKES 4-6 SERVINGS

2 cups frozen peas

1 tablespoon chopped fresh mint leaves

1 tablespoon unsalted butter, cut into pieces

Salt

Put about ½ inch of water in a medium saucepan, add the peas, and cover. Set the pan over high heat and bring to a boil. Reduce the heat to medium and simmer until the peas are just tender, 4 to 5 minutes.

Pour the peas into a colander set in the sink. Drain well—shaking the colander helps—and return the peas to the saucepan over medium heat. Add the mint, butter, and several pinches of salt and stir until the butter melts. Transfer to a bowl and serve right away.

Roasted Carrots

Sweet roasted carrots are a terrific accompaniment to almost any main course—that is, if you don't eat all of them before they make it to the table! Try to find multicolored carrots, sold in bunches, for a fun, festive-looking side dish.

MAKES 4 SERVINGS

1 pound carrots, trimmed

1 tablespoon unsalted butter, cut into little pieces

2 tablespoons brown sugar

¼ teaspoon ground ginger

½ teaspoon salt

Ground black pepper

Preheat the oven to 400°F.

Peel the carrots and cut them crosswise into thirds. Cut each piece in half lengthwise, and then cut any extra-thick pieces in half lengthwise again, forming wedges. Place the carrots in an even layer on a rimmed baking sheet and dot with the butter.

Roast the carrots, stirring occasionally, until tender and beginning to brown, about 30 minutes.

While the carrots are roasting, in a small bowl, stir together the brown sugar, ginger, and salt.

Remove the baking sheet from the oven. Sprinkle the carrots evenly with the sugar mixture. Return the baking sheet to the oven and continue to roast the carrots until the sugar is melted and syrupy, about 5 minutes.

Remove the baking sheet from the oven and transfer the carrots to a platter or bowl. Season with pepper. Serve right away.

Roasted veggies

Swap out the cauliflower for asparagus spears or broccoli florets and roast in the same way.

Roasted Cauliflower

Roasting vegetables in a hot oven caramelizes their natural sugars and brings out a rich, nutty sweetness. If you like, substitute chopped cooked bacon, chopped olives, or currants for the lemon zest that's tossed in just before serving.

MAKES 6-8 SERVINGS

1 head cauliflower (about 1½ pounds)

3 tablespoons olive oil

½ teaspoon salt

Grated zest of 1 lemon

Preheat the oven to 425°F.

Trim off and discard the green outer leaves, and then cut the cauliflower from top to bottom into quarters. Cut out the core from each quarter, and then cut the cauliflower into medium florets.

Arrange the cauliflower in a single layer on a rimmed baking sheet and drizzle with the olive oil. Sprinkle with the salt and toss until the florets are evenly coated with oil.

Roast the cauliflower until golden on the bottom, about 15 minutes. Remove the baking sheet from the oven and use a wide metal spatula to turn over the florets. Continue to roast until tender and golden on the second sides, 10 to 15 minutes longer.

Remove the baking sheet from the oven and transfer the cauliflower to a platter. Sprinkle with the lemon zest, toss to combine, and serve right away.

Index

weldon**owen**

P.O. Box 3088, San Rafael, CA 94912
www.weldonowen.com

WELDON OWEN INTERNATIONAL
President & Publisher Roger Shaw
VP, Sales & Marketing Amy Kaneko
Finance Manager Philip Paulick
Associate Publisher Amy Marr
Project Editor Kim Laidlaw
Associate Editor Emma Rudolph
Creative Director Kelly Booth
Associate Art Director Lisa Berman
Original Design Alexandra Zeigler
Senior Production Designer Rachel Lopez Metzger
Production Director Chris Hemesath
Associate Production Director Michelle Duggan
Production Manager Michelle Woo
Director of Enterprise Systems Shawn Macey
Imaging Manager Don Hill
Photographer Nicole Hill Gerulat
Food Stylist Marian Cooper Cairns
Prop Stylist Veronica Olson
Hair & Makeup Kathy Hill

AMERICAN GIRL *COOKING*
Conceived and produced by Weldon Owen International
In collaboration with Williams Sonoma, Inc.
3250 Van Ness Avenue, San Francisco, CA 94109

Printed in the China

First printed in 2016
10 9 8 7 6 5 4 3 2 1

Library of Congress Cataloging in Publication
data is available

ISBN: 978-1-68188-101-0

ACKNOWLEDGMENTS
Weldon Owen wishes to thank the following people for their generous support to help produce this book: David Bornfriend, Pranavi Chopra, Nina & Dan Fife, Shauna Green, Jessica Howell, Christine Lee, Kristene Loayza, Rachel Markowitz, Hristina Misafiris, Jacob Muai, Taylor Olson, Elizabeth Parson, Heather Siembieda, Abby Stolfo, and Dawn Yanagihara

A VERY SPECIAL THANK YOU TO:
Our models: Kailee Bauer, Aeslin Cameron, Georgia Faith, Nathaniel Floyd, Jaden Fode, Hadley Hayes, Ruby Nash, Jasmyn Ramos, Ariela Salas, Sadhana Som

Our locations: The Goodmans, The Parkers, The Swaners
Our party resources: Julie Bluét, Rice by Rice, Shop Sweet Lulu, The Sugar Diva, Tea Collection
Our clothing resources: Rachel Riley (rachelriley.com) and Tea Collection (teacollection.com)

Collect Them All

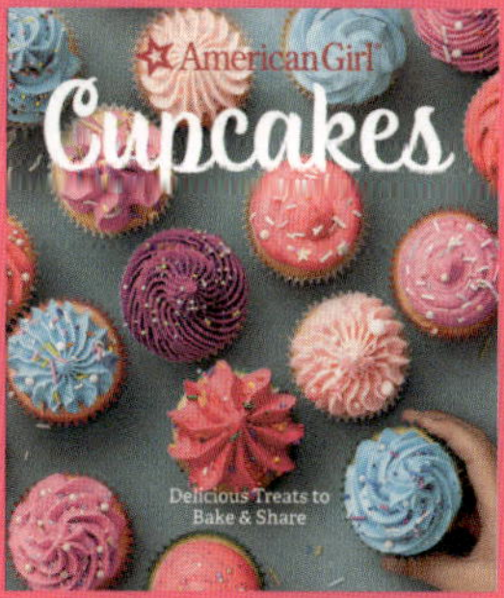